Winning Souls For Christ:

A Guide for Teens and Young Adults

Guided Curriculum

Althea Jones

Ordering Information

For quantity sales, special discounts may be available for corporations, associations, and others; contact the author at theajdon@gmail.com.

Editor & Consultant

Lita P. Ward, The Editorial Midwife
LPW Editing & Consulting Services, LLC
Editorial Midwife Publishing
www.litaward.org / lpwediting@gmail.com

Printed in USA

Dear Leaders, Parents, and Sunday School Teachers,

It Is with great pleasure that I share this "Winning Souls For Christ: A Guide For Teens and Young Adults" curriculum with you. I have created a curriculum for this guide because I have had the opportunity to work with youth and young adults for years. I was also a youth once in high school who shared and started her journey learning and living for Christ. I have witnessed a great transformation, and I understand the importance of following after Christ while not succumbing to the pressures of life and the world.

"Winning Souls For Christ" is a guide specialized for teens and young adults. Still, one I believe can assist adults in reaching the lives and hearts of our younger generation who may have lost their way. "Winning Souls For Christ: A Guide for Teens and Young Adults" book was first written and published in 2018, where I shared my personal testimony, having a relationship with Christ, being a witness to other youth, being a witness through our lifestyle and character, and where I shared do's and don't while being an example for Christ.

Since then, I've taken the time to revise the book, "Winning Souls For Christ: A Guide for Teens and Young Adults," which was published in November 2021. In this version, I go a little deeper, share my testimony, and explain how it relates to our purpose in Christ. I also share and define the word *soul* and how that helps make us who we are. I share about our Father and how He has purpose for us, but Satan also has a purpose: to steal, kill, and destroy.

This curriculum I have created can be used during Vacation Bible School, Sunday School, Teen and Young Adult groups, or even through Teen and Young Adult Hubs. Through this curriculum, I have laid a foundation for specific areas and questions accompanying the book. It can be used for eight (8) weeks after every Chapter or over the course of 12 weeks, which gives the readers a chance to read the story and engage in the activities, questions, and resources provided.

I believe, like never before, that Christ must be the foundation. Darkness has a significant influence, but now is the time for the Kingdom of Light to rise above the influence of darkness. God has a remnant, a small minority of believers He is raising. Our Father has called youth; they are strong! He will give them the ability to mount up like wings as eagles and be a powerful influence when their heart is tender before Him. I wholeheartedly believe this curriculum will help the reader understand and engage in the message through the book.

I hope you see growth and excitement in the lives of those you teach after you use this curriculum. Using these resources to their fullest capacity can positively influence the hearts and lives of those around you!

Sincerely,

Althea C. Jones

Table of Contents

Lesson One: "The Soul"

In today's lesson, we will talk about the soul. Scriptures are provided for reference, and questions to be discussed at the end of the lesson. Our soul develops when we are conceived in our mother's womb. Our soul is our makeup. It is what generates our character, our decisions, our thinking, feelings, and emotions. Our soul is important to Christ because God created and formed us. *And the LORD God formed man of the dust of the ground, and breathed into his nostrils the breath of life; and man became a living soul* (Genesis 2:7).

It is important to our Father that our soul is in good health and prospers. However, for these results, we must give our lives to Christ so He can direct our paths and order our steps.

Scripture References

Matthew 16:26 - *For what is a man profited, if he shall gain the whole world, and lose his own soul? Or what shall a man give in exchange for his soul?*

Matthew 22:37 - *Jesus said unto him, Thou shalt love the Lord thy God with all thy heart, and with all thy soul, and with all thy mind.*

3 John 1:2 - *Beloved, I wish above all things that thou mayest prosper and be in health, even as thy soul prospereth.*

Guided Activity

Lesson One: "Soul Diagram"

Materials: Large paper, Markers

Directions: Form groups of two; have one person be A and the other B. Person A lays on the paper while person B draws around them, tracing their layout. After the diagram is drawn, students draw a divided line in the middle and label each side as "Corrupt and Uncorrupt." Have partners discuss what they have experienced or know that has corrupted their souls, things that want to corrupt them, and how they can improve their souls.

Discussion Questions

1. When you hear the word *soul*, what does that mean to you? (Turn to the book's first page of the Introduction to Dialogue.)

2. What does our soul mean to Christ? (Think about it and discuss it with a partner, then share.)

3. How does Christ win someone's soul?

4. What are some ways your soul can be corrupted? What are some major influences that have an impact on your soul?

Lesson One Review

1. Our souls begin to develop when _____ .

2. Our souls generate our _____, _____, _____, _____, and _____ .

3. Genesis 2:7 - And the Lord God formed man of the _____ from the ground and breathed into his nostrils the _____ of _____; and man became a living _____ .

4. 3 John 1:2 - Beloved, I wish above all things that mayest prosper and be in _____, even as thy _____ _____ .

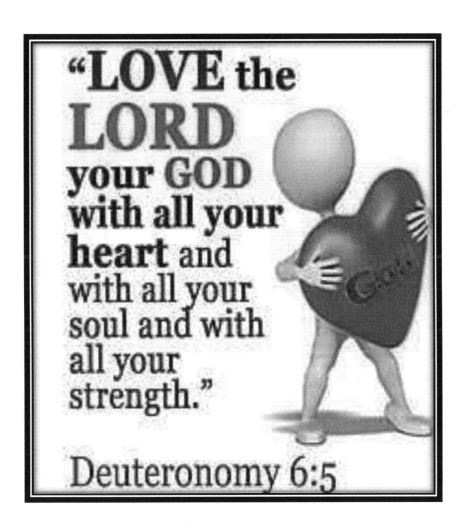

"LOVE the LORD your GOD with all your heart and with all your soul and with all your strength."

Deuteronomy 6:5

NOTES

Lesson Two: Unique and Distinct
(Read Chapter 1, Part 1)

God created each of you and formed you in your mother's womb. He knew you before you were even there. Jeremiah 1:5 says, *Before I formed thee in the belly I knew thee; and before thou camest forth out of the womb I sanctified thee, and I ordained thee a prophet unto the nations.*

You each have a unique way about yourself and are distinct, set apart, and different. God created man in His image, which should always bring glory back to Him. *So God created man in his own image, in the image of God created he him; male and female created he them* (Genesis 1:27). Although the world has a corrupted image, God's image is beauty and splendor.

<u>Scripture References</u>

Matthew 10:30 - *But the very hairs of your head are numbered* ~ **By Christ.**

You, beloved, are… 1 Peter 2:9 - *But ye are a chosen generation, holy nation, royal priesthood: a peculiar people, that ye should shew forth the praises of him who hath called you out of darkness into his marvelous light:*

Guided Activity

Lesson Two: "Unique and Distinct"

Materials: Bibles, Popsicle Sticks, Glue, Foil to Reflect as a Mirror

Directions: Have the group make mirrors using four popsicle sticks, glue, and foil. After pieces are placed together, groups work together to create "I" Statements using Scriptures about being uniquely made, their heart, mind, or soul. Then, use these statements to write around the border of the mirror they created.

Examples:

1. *I am uniquely made.*
2. *I am beautifully and wonderfully made.*
3. *My soul is…*
4. *I have purpose because…*

Discussion Questions

1. What are some of your strengths? What are some weaknesses?

2. As a child, what were some things that made you different from everyone else?

3. What have you noticed as a teenager and young adult that makes you different?

4. What do you like most about yourself?

"Fall in love with what God created!" ~ Althea Jones

Lesson Two Review

1. God created man in _____ _____ _____, in the image of God created he him; _____ and _____ he created them.

2. 1 Peter 2:9 – "But ye are a _____ _____, a _____ _____, an _____ _____, a _____ _____; that ye should shew forth the praises of him who hath called you out of darkness into his marvellous light;"

3. Define the word *distinct*.

4. Define the word *peculiar*.

5. Define the word *unique*.

NOTES

Lesson Three: Your Purpose
(Read Chapter 1, Part 2)

Our purpose began in the beginning. God created us to have dominion over all that was created. He intended for us to tend to His garden where all we needed would be, starting with Adam and Eve (Genesis 1:25-30).

Our purpose comes from God. He gave us purpose when He thought of us before we were in our mother's womb. For you to live your purpose, you must live for Him. Your purpose begins to unfold as a little child. There are things that you will find yourself interested in that are tied to your purpose.

Scripture References

Proverbs 16:3 - *Commit thy works unto the Lord, and thy thoughts shall be established.* When we commit our works, lives, and ourselves to the Lord, He will make known His purpose for us.

Job 23:14 - *For he performeth the thing that is appointed for me: and many such things are with him.* You have a purpose.

Romans 11:29 - *For the gifts and calling of God are without repentance.*

Guided Activity

Lesson Three: "Purpose"

Materials: Stickers, Markers, Crayons, Colored Pencils, Glue and/or Tape, Poster Boards (Small or Large), Magazines and/or Newspapers

Directions: Create Goals or Vision Boards. Create 2–3 month goals that can be accomplished or 1-3-year vision boards.

Discussion Questions

1. What is the definition of *Purpose*?

2. Can you remember something that you were interested in as a child? (Take a moment, think and share.)

3. Are you doing what you were interested in now or something similar?

4. How can you clearly find out what your purpose is?

5. What does the Holy Ghost represent? What does the Holy Ghost give you the ability to do?

6. When you are confused about your purpose, what should you do?

7. What can detour your purpose?

"Purpose begins the moment you say Yes to Christ." ~ *Althea Jones*

Lesson Three Review

1. The Holy Ghost represents _____. (Page 3)

2. The Holy Ghost gives you the ability to do the _____ of the Father. (Page 3)

3. The Holy Ghost gives you _____ after you receive. (Acts 1:8)

4. For you to live your purpose, you must _____ for Christ.

5. Purpose begins to unfold as a _____ _____.

6. Purpose begins the moment you say _____ to Christ.

GOD MADE
YOU FOR A
PURPOSE...
FIND IT

NOTES

Lesson Four: Testimonies

Testimonies are stories we share that represent overcoming obstacles or challenges. Testimonies of Christ represent stories we share where God gave us strength to overcome or when He saved us. They are stories we share that share His goodness towards us. They share and tell of experiences. Testimonies share the Word or Words of the Lord.

Testimonies - Affirmations or declarations made towards God.

Scripture References

Luke 8:39 - *Return to thine own house, and shew how great things God hath done unto thee. And he went his way, and published throughout the whole city how great things Jesus had done unto him.*

2 Timothy 1:8 - *Be not thou therefore ashamed of the testimony of our Lord, nor of me his prisoner: but be thou partaker of the afflictions of the gospel according to the power of God;*

Revelation 12:11 - *And they overcame him by the blood of the Lamb, and by the word of their testimony; and they loved not their lives unto the death.*

Guided Activity

Lesson Four: "Testimonies"

Materials: 8-10 chairs placed in a circle.

Directions: Dialogue and share testimonies, something you have overcome or maybe praying to overcome. End this activity by having the group pray for each other!

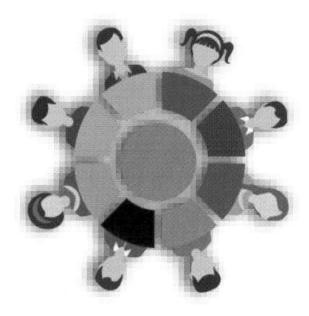

Discussion Questions

(Note: Read Chapter 1, Part 3/ Pages 7-15.)

1. What challenges have you faced as a youth or young adult?

2. What are some challenges you have overcome?

3. Take a moment to share a testimony.

Lesson Four Review

1. Testimonies are _____ .

2. The definition of *yoke* is _____ .
   (Refer to Page 12.)

3. Should you be ashamed of the testimonies of God? _____ (Yes or No)

4. Testimonies share and tell _____

   _____

   _____

   _____ .

"Declare that Christ is Lord. We overcome by speaking, sharing, and telling the good that God is doing." ~ Althea Jones

TESTIMONIES

And they overcame him by the blood of the Lamb and by the word of their testimony, and they did not love their lives to the death. Revelation 12:11 (NKJV)

NOTES

Lesson Five: "Being Born Again"

To be born again, you must be birthed into a newness in Christ. You must be birthed in the Spirit. This is where you have dedicated your life to Christ and have decided to live for Him by laying down your own wants, desires, and will. To be born in Christ, you must renounce your own ways of living to take on His ways. This means to live out of His Spirit. To also live out His nature and character and represent the Word of God. Being born again is to be born to represent the Kingdom of the Father. As a young adult, this is possible. His strength is made whole in your weakness. *But he said to me, "My grace is sufficient for you, for my power is made perfect in weakness"* (2 Corinthians 12:8).

Scripture References

John 3:3 - *Jesus answered and said unto him, Verily, verily, I say unto thee, Except a man be born again, he cannot see the kingdom of God.*

1 Peter 1:23 - *Being born again, not of corruptible seed, but of incorruptible, by the word of God, which liveth and abideth for ever.*

Guided Activity

Lesson Five: "Born Again"

Materials: Props to Recreate Nicodemus and Jesus' conversation (costumes, two chairs, etc.) Be creative!

Directions: Role-play the conversation between Nicodemus and Jesus. Create a commercial or website ad acting out their conversation.

Discussion Questions

1. When you think about being birthed again, what do you imagine that to look like?

2. Do you believe being born again is a new way of life? Why or why not?

3. Why is it important to allow God to change your thinking after being born again?

4. What can help you form an intimate relationship with Christ?

"It's time to step out of your comfort zone to step into the things of Christ."
Althea Jones

Lesson Five Review

1. To be born again, you must be _____ .

2. The process starts with _____ and getting rid of things that take you away from _____ . (See Page 16.)

3. Being born again is a _____ in Christ. (See Page 16.)

4. Does a person experience ***change*** or ***stay the same*** during the process of being born again?

Jesus Talks With Nicodemus

Ye Must Be Born Again

John 3:1- *There was a man of the Pharisees, named Nicodemus, a ruler of the Jews: he same came to Jesus by night, and said unto him, Rabbi, we know that thou art a teacher come from God: for no man can do these miracles that thou doest, except God be with him. Jesus answered and said unto him, Verily, verily, I say unto thee, Except a man be born again, he cannot see the kingdom of God.*
4 Nicodemus saith unto him, How can a man be born when he is old? can he enter the second time into his mother's womb, and be born? Jesus answered, Verily, verily, I say unto thee, Except a man be born of water and of the Spirit, he cannot enter into the kingdom of God.

29

NOTES

Lesson Six: "Being a Witness"
(Read Isaiah 43:1-10)

When we become witnesses for God, we are responsible for speaking of His goodness and sharing testimonies of what He has done in our lives. God wants us to be effective in our witness; He wants us to witness so that change can begin to occur in the individuals we are speaking to. God has broken barriers in your life and wants to do the same thing for someone you know who is in your life or will be coming into your life.

<u>Scripture References</u>

Isaiah 43:10 - *Ye are my witnesses, saith the Lord, and my servant whom I have chosen: that ye may know and believe me, and understand that I am he: before me there was no God formed, neither shall there be after me.*

Matthew 5:16 - *Let your light so shine before men, that they may see your good works, and glorify your Father which is in heaven.*

Guided Activity

Lesson Six: "Being a Witness"

Materials: Chairs formed into a circle.

Directions: Play the game of telephone. Have one student whisper a scripture until it gets to the end of the circle. Let's see if it makes it to the last ear and correctly recited!

Discussion Questions

1. Think about those you could witness to in your life. Who are they?

2. Why would it be important to witness to these people?

3. Why is it important for you to be a great witness? (See Page 29.)

4. Name three ways that you can witness. (See Page 26.)

Lesson Six Review

1. Define the definitions of _being a witness and witnessing_.

   _____

   _____

   _____

   _____

   _____

   _____

   _____

2. Witnessing can be done through _____, _____,

   _____, _____ and _____,

   and _____.

3. Our impact comes through _____. (See Page 26.)

4. Witnessing means you are being _____.

   A. A Compromiser

   B. A Liar

   C. An Example

Luke 4:43 - *But he said, "I must proclaim the good news of the kingdom of God to the other towns also, because that is why I was sent."*

NOTES

Lesson Seven: " Being an Example"

Every day we live, we are supposed to be examples. In all that we do, from how we think down to how we act and carry ourselves. When you become a witness, you set the stage for representing Christ in every way. You are living to display the image and character of your Father and Savior. You are living to demonstrate the characteristics of God to the world, which shines brighter than any display ever known. While you are the vessel being used, God is the source of your strength, and we have been created to be the lights of this world.

Scripture Reference

Matthew 5: 13-16

13 *Ye are the salt of the earth: but if the salt have lost his savour, wherewith shall it be salted? it is thenceforth good for nothing, but to be cast out, and to be trodden under foot of men.*

14 *Ye are the light of the world. A city that is set on an hill cannot be hid.*

15 *Neither do men light a candle, and put it under a bushel, but on a candlestick; and it giveth light unto all that are in the house.*

16 *Let your light so shine before men, that they may see your good works, and glorify your Father which is in heaven.*

Guided Activity

Lesson Seven: "Examples"

Materials: Paper and Notepad

Directions: Set your own goals to meet a few friends next week. Write down the number you wish to meet and how you hope to witness to them. Note whether your form of witness will be by sending them a song, a scripture, or calling them to pray with them.

Discussion Questions

1. Define the word *example*.

2. When you hear the word *compromise*, what does that mean to you?

3. Being an example is very similar to being a witness. Describe how you could be an effective example in your classroom, at home, at work, in restaurants, or wherever you are?

4. Name some characteristics of God that would make you an effective example.

5. Why is it important to be an effective example?

Lesson Seven Review

1. To be an example for Christ is to be more like Him. It's _____, _____, and _____. It's being and making an _____. (See Page 39.)

2. God loves intimacy. When we spend intentional time with Him, He lets us know precisely _____ to do and _____ to do it. (See Page 39.)

3. Being an example isn't _____, but falling deeper into the palms of our _____ Father. (See Page 38.)

You are the light
of the world.

Matthew 5:14

NOTES

Lesson Eight: "Satan's Plans" -
New Age Practices & Distractions

Satan's tactics are to use things to entice you. His plans are to distract you because of your thoughts, feelings, and thinking. His plans are to destroy your life before you can understand his disguise. He uses those around you, the things you like, and what he knows will make you feel those feelings you desire. His plans are to get you tangled up, bound, and yoked to dysfunction and lies so that you can think God is the one who isn't for you. He plans to feed you deception because he knows it's what you will believe. Satan uses your friends, social media, false truths, and socioeconomic status. His plans are for you to see life from a worldly perspective, not a kingdom perspective. He wants you to feel like you can do all things on your own when, in reality, he knows if you fall in love with Christ, you will see what real life, love, and living are all about. His plans are for you to agree with spirits of darkness while you aren't even aware of what you are doing. He wants to get you and your mind so far away from seeking and hearing the voice of the Father. He uses what you like, what you feel you need, and what looks right. Don't fall for his plans; it leads to destruction.

<u>Scripture Reference</u>

John 10:10 - *The thief comes only to steal and kill and destroy. I came that they may have life and have it abundantly.*

Guided Activity

Chapter Eight: Satan's Plans

Materials: The Bible

Directions: Dialogue about New Age Practices and Distractions. Make diagrams of "New Age versus Christ's Desires." Share some struggles and distractions that you have faced. End this activity with prayers!

Homework: Write down any questions that you may have and bring them to the next study.

Discussion Questions

1. What are new age practices? How can they detour you from serving Christ?

2. In John 10:10, Jesus came to give us life and life more abundantly. What does _a more abundant life_ mean to you?

3. Identify some distractions in your own life. Have they kept you from praying or spending time with God? What can you do differently to spend more time with God?

4. Think about the friends in your world. Have they ever distracted you from doing the right things? Something or someone who distracts you, would you describe them as good?

Lesson Eight Review

1. Satan's tactics are to use things that _____ you.

2. His plans are to get you _____ up, _____, and _____ to dysfunction and _____ so that you can think God is the one who isn't for you.

3. His plans are for you to agree to with _____ _____ _____ while you aren't even aware of what you are doing.

4. John 10:10 The _____ comes only to _____ and _____ and _____. I came that you may have _____ and have it _____.

NOTES

Lesson Nine: "Ask Questions"

You are in a time where you are developing, growing, learning, and experiencing. You will have times when you have questions. As a growing believer, it is totally okay to ask any question you have to someone who can answer those questions wisely. God wants us to better understand what He's saying and what He has said in His Word. It is not okay for you to be confused, nor is it okay for you to have a question and feel like you can't ask. When we fully understand the Word of God and the things of God, we can live in His truth and in His promises. We can live as His true sons and daughters. God wants us to know the truth because He wants us to live liberally in Him by the power of His Spirit. God wants you and I to live as His chosen generation; He also wants us to live freely and to operate correctly.

Scripture Reference

James 1:5 (NIV) - *If any of you lack wisdom, you should ask God, who gives generously to all without finding fault, and it will be given to you.*

Guided Activity

Lesson Nine: "Ask Questions!"

Materials: Use the homework assignment from Lesson Eight and the Bible.

Directions: Swap questions, share, and dialogue.

Discussion Question

What questions do you have? (Use this section for open discussion.)

<u>Lesson Nine Review</u>

1. Why is it important to ask questions?

2. When we fully understand the _____ and the things of God, we
    can live in His _____ and in His _____.

NOTES

Lesson Ten: " Don't Be Afraid"

As children of God, when you carry the Spirit of God, it isn't with fear. God's Spirit fills us with a fullness of joy, power, and boldness. God intends for us to be bold through the power of his might. He didn't intend for us to walk in fear. How can we say we trust God and fear at the same time? As humans, we experience fear from not knowing the outcomes of a particular thing or situation. Still, we can't allow fear to intimidate us, causing us to be disobedient. While fear is a natural emotion, we must distinguish between natural fear and the spirit of fear. The spirit of fear comes to rob and cause torment from the assignments and responsibilities you have from God. God wants us to rely upon Him and walk in His Spirit of victory. We have a Father who will go before us. Fear causes stagnation; it also causes compromise, and when you walk in fear, you walk away from going after the will and purposes of God.

Scripture Reference

2 Timothy 1:7 - *For God hath not given us the spirit of fear; but of power, and of love, and of a sound mind.*

Guided Activity

Lesson Ten: "Don't Be Afraid!"

Materials: Bible and Blindfolds

Directions: "Fight or Flight… Is Fear Good or Bad?"

Have the group pick partners and blindfold one while the other stands behind them. The blindfolded person must try to trust their partner to not allow them to fall. Use a timer of about three seconds and tell those blindfolded to fall back while relying on their partner to catch them. Switch and begin again. Dialogue when finished. How did that feel? Did they genuinely trust their partner? Discuss why it's important to trust God and ways to let go of their own control to build trust in God.

Discussion Question

1. What is the definition of fear?

2. Think of a time when you were told to do something but allowed fear to stop you. Share and tell how it made you feel.

3. Why is it important not to fear and be obedient?

4. What do you receive God's power through?

5. What is the spirit of fear? What can a spirit of fear cause?

Lesson Ten Review

1. God intends for us to be _____ through the _____ of His might.

2. While fear is a _____ _____, we have to _____ between natural fear and the _____ _____ _____.

3. The spirit of fear comes to _____ and causes _____ from the assignments and responsibilities that you have from God.

4. God's Spirit fills us with a fullness of _____, _____, and _____.

NOTES

Lesson Eleven: "Processes"

Processes are for growth and maturity. They are to teach, help, and cause us to come into a place of fullness in God. Processes help us to see ourselves, where we are, and where we are not. Processes can be good, and some can be challenging. Processes are meant to help us get to where we are meant to be. Processes help us because they give God room to groom His bride. It gives Him room to liberate us, make and mold us into His very own image. God is the surgeon of our souls. He's the one who knows what is in us and what needs to come out.

As you grow older, you will go through processes. There will be learning processes, needing understanding and making decisions, whether good or bad; in all processes, there is experience. No matter the experience of processes, God's plans for you matter most. His plans are what will take you to the place where you are meant to be. All processes are for your learning, maturing, and growing. Go through them and learn to become better. Learn to become greater! Learn to become who you are meant to be!

Scripture Reference

Isaiah 41:10 (NIV) - *So do not fear, for I am with you; ... do not be dismayed, for I am your God. I will strengthen you and help you; I will uphold you with my righteous right hand.*

Guided Activity

Lesson Eleven: "Processes"

Materials: Four Small Balls

Directions: Have the whole group split into two groups. Begin the group by giving directions that they will throw one ball by choosing someone to throw to within that circle. They are to create a cycle: when one ball has reached everyone, the next ball is added until they have reached all four balls. After they have thrown all four balls, they will reverse by starting with the last person who received the ball, repeating the cycle they initially began with, and ending with the very first person. They will add each ball every time the ball reaches the first person; they begin the game with a new ball. They will begin the process by starting normally and then reversing the cycle to see if they can remember the process in which the balls were thrown.

At the end of the activity, dialogue about processes. How did that feel? What are processes like? How do processes help? Did it cause you to focus, to be confused, etc.?

<u>Discussion Questions</u>

1. What is your definition of the word *process*?

2. As a teenager and young adult, what processes have you learned from?

3. What lessons did you learn?

4. Why are processes good?

5. What are four words that describe change that happens to us through processes? (See Page 59.)

Lesson Eleven Review

1. Processes are for _____ and _____.

2. They are to _____, _____ and cause us to come into a place of _____ in God.

3. God is the _____ of our _____.

4. Processes can be _____ and some can be _____.

5. Processes are for your _____, _____, and _____.

NOTES

Lesson Review Answer Key

Lesson One

1. Our souls begin to develop when ***we are conceived in our mother's womb***.

2. Our soul generates our ***character, decisions, thinking, feelings, and emotions***.

3. Genesis 2:7 - And the Lord God formed man of the ***dust*** of the ground, and breathed into his nostrils the ***breath*** of ***life***; and man became a living ***soul***.

4. 3 John 1:2 - Beloved, I wish above all things that mayest prosper and be ***in health***, even as thy ***soul prospereth***.

Lesson Two

1. God created man in ***his own image***, in the image of God created he him; ***male*** and ***female*** he created them. (Genesis 1:27 KJV)

2. 1 Peter 2:9 - But ye are a ***chosen generation***, ***a royal priesthood***, ***an holy nation***, ***a peculiar people***; that ye should shew forth the praises of him who hath called you out of darkness into his marvellous light;

3. Define the word ***distinct***.

A. Literally, having the difference marked separated by a visible sign, or by a note or mark, as a place distinct by a name. (KJV Bible Dictionary)
B. Recognizably different in nature from something else of a similar type.

4. Define the word *peculiar*.

    Appropriate, belonging to a person and only him (KJV Bible Dictionary)

5. Define the word *unique*.

    Being the only one of its kind, unlike anything else.

Lesson Three

1. The Holy Ghost represents *Christ's Spirit*.

2. The Holy Ghost gives you the ability to do the *will* of the Father.

3. The Holy Ghost gives you *power* after you receive. (Acts 1:8_

4. For you to live your purpose, you must *live* for Christ.

5. Purpose begins to unfold as a *little child*.

6. Purpose begins the moment you say *yes* to Christ.

Lesson Four

1. Testimonies are ***stories we share about overcoming***.

2. The definition of yoke is ***a mark of servitude, slavery, bondage, or a chain, a link, a bond of connection***. (Refer to page 12.)

3. Should you be ashamed of the testimonies of God? ***No***

4. Testimonies share and tell ***experiences***.

Lesson Five

1. To be born again, you must be ***birthed into newness in Christ.***

2. The process starts with ***us maturing*** and getting rid of things that take you away from ***Christ***. (See page 16.)

3. Being born again is a ***spiritual birthing*** in Christ. (See page 16.)

   Does a person experience ***change*** or ***stay the same*** during the process of being born again? ***A person experience change during the process.***

Lesson Six

1. Define the definition of witness and witnessing. ***Seeing in persons, bearing testimony, and giving testimony.***

2. Witnessing can be done through ***evangelizing***, ***teaching***, ***ministering***, ***personal businesses*** and ***establishments***, and ***praying with and for others***. (See Page 28.)

3. Our impact comes through ***God***. (See Page 26.)

4. Witnessing means you are being _____.
   A. A Compromiser
   B. A Liar
   C. An Example

Lesson Seven

1. To be an example for Christ is to be more like Him. It's ***expressing***, ***showing***, and ***telling***. It's being and making an ***impact***. (See Page 39.)

2. God loves intimacy. When we spend intentional time with Him, He lets us know precisely ***what*** to do and ***when*** to do it. (See Page 39.)

3. Being an example isn't ***compromising*** but falling deeper into the palms of our ***loving*** Father. (See Page 38.)

Lesson Eight

1. Satan's tactics are to use things to **_entice_** you.

2. His plans are to get you **_tangled_** up, **_bound_**, and **_yoked_** to dysfunction and **_lies_** so that you can think God is the one who isn't for you.

3. His plans are for you to agree with **_spirits of darkness_** while you aren't even aware of what you are doing.

4. John 10:10 - The **_thief_** comes only to **_steal_** and **_kill_** and **_destroy_**. I came that you may have **_life_** and have it **_abundantly_**.

Lesson Nine

1. Why is it important to ask questions? (See Page 46-47.)

Possible Answers:

- *God wants us to hear and live by understanding.*
- *God wants us to know who He is and biblical history that helps us understand what His Word is saying and how it applies to the times we are living in right now.*
- *God wants us to live liberally in Him.*
- *When you ask questions, you can find out who the Father is, and you can find out how He operates and how He sees you.*

5. When we fully understand the **_Word of God_** and the things of God, we can live in His **_truth_** and in His **_promises_**.

Lesson Ten

1. God intends for us to be **_bold_** through the **_power_** of His might.

2. While fear is a **_natural emotion,_** we have to **_distinguish_** between natural fear and the **_spirit of fear_**.

3. The spirit of fear comes to **_rob_** and causes **_torment_** from the assignments and responsibilities that you have from God.

6. God's Spirit fills us with a fullness of **_joy_**, **_power_**, and **_boldness_**.

Lesson Eleven

1. Processes are for **_growth_** and **_maturity_**.

2. They are to **_teach_**, **_help_**, and cause us to come into a place of **_fullness_** in God.

3. God is the **_surgeon_** of our **_souls_**.
4. Processes can be **_good_** and some can be **_challenging_**.

5. Processes are for your **_learning_**, **_maturing_**, and **_growing_**.

Meet The Author

Winning Souls For Christ: A Guide For Teens and Young Adults book was written to teach, demonstrate, share, influence, and impact teens and young adults. It was written to reach those with a heart of youth.

Althea started writing in middle school. She was inspired as a teenager to write her book, the first version of Winning Souls For Christ, and later led by God to revise it after she learned more and experienced working with teens and young adults. She wrote it to share her personal experiences while also sharing wisdom to help teens, and young adults understand that falling in love with Christ is personal, that Christ has called them, and that He loves them and wants to use them.

She created this guided curriculum in conjunction with her book. The intent and purpose of the guide are to be used within groups and among young people. She included lessons, discussions, and reviews, giving the facilitator a chance to gather youth, teach them about Christ, talk with them, and give them a chance to be in a safe space where they are gathered and can build relationships.

Althea's passion and desire is to be a barrier breaker in the lives of teens and young adults. She is a mother of 3 sons and works in education as a School Counselor. While she understands that many teens face peer pressure daily from what they see, hear, and are told, this guide is created to gather, teach, and give them a community to learn and hear more about Christ.

Althea believes that impartation is essential. However, to get results, it's important to understand that change doesn't happen overnight. She believes that youth are the "NEXT" generation and that God is pouring his Spirit out right now for youth to rise and be bold while overcoming temptation and peer pressure!

She has written five books *"Winning Souls For Christ: A Guide For Teens and Young Adults," Winning Souls For Christ: A Guide For Teens and Young Adults (Revised), Counting My Blessings (Reflection Journal), "I Can Because I Am" and Winning Souls for Christ A Guide For Teens and Young Adults: Guided Curriculum.*

For More Information

Contact Althea through Social Media or email:

Facebook: Althea Jones (Purposed Writing)

Instagram: Althea Jones

Email: altheajones3@yahoo.com

Made in the USA
Columbia, SC
10 February 2024

31370469R00046